흙과 흙이 합쳐지고
물과 물이 하나되네

Soil Joins Soil, Water Joins Water, To Become One

사 진 으 로   보 는   2 0 0 7   남 북 정 상 회 담

기획 **국정홍보처** | 글 **손동우** | 사진 **2007 남북정상회담 사진공동취재단**

흙과 흙이 합쳐지고
물과 물이 하나되네

바다출판사

사진은 역사를 바꾼다

조정래(소설가)

역사는 생명 있는 모든 것들의 삶이다. 그런데 역사는 '기록'이 되어야만 비로소 완전한 제 모습을 갖춘다. 그러므로 역사는 인간만이 지니는 고유한 발명품이다. 인간만이 기록의 도구인 문자를 소유한 까닭이다.

그런데 인간은 문자로 그치지 않았다. 또 하나 기록의 도구를 갖추었다. 그것이 사진이다. 사진의 효과는 때때로 문학을, 미술을, 음악을 절망시킬 때가 있다. 자연 현상의 기기묘묘한 절묘함 앞에서 수많은 미술가와 문학가와 음악가 들은 자기들의 표현 능력 부족을 절감하며 절망하고는 한다. 그런데 사진은 전혀 절망함이 없이 그 기능을 뽐낸다.

사진은 표현 기능만 탁월한 것이 아니다. 한 장의 사진은 때로 역사를 바꾸기도 한다. 남자, 여자, 노인, 어린아이 할 것 없이 모두 발가벗겨진 알몸으로 가스실로 끌려 들어가는 모습. 그 한 장의 사진이 없었다면 전 인류는 나치의 죄상에 그렇게 치를 떨지 못했을 것이다. 시체를 열 겹, 스무 겹 장작 쌓아올리듯이 해서 매장한 현장. 그 한 장의 사진이 없었더라면 일본의 '남경 학살' 부인은 그대로 통했을 것이다. 이처럼 사진의 역사 기록성은 가끔씩 문자를 능가하고 압도한다.

6·15 남북공동선언은 분단시대를 통일시대로 바꾼 전환점이었다. 그것을 토대로 하

여 이루어진 '2007 남북정상회담'은 우리 민족이 평화통일의 고속도로를 닦기 시작한 큰 성과이다. 그 회담이 낳은 선언서의 제목은 '남북관계 발전과 평화번영을 위한 선언'이다. 통일은 우리 민족이 반드시 풀어야 할 숙원이고 비원이다. 그런데 그 방법을 전쟁이 없는 '평화번영'을 통해 하자고 남북 두 정상은 칠천만 민족 앞에, 그리고 세계를 향하여 선언한 것이다. 이 얼마나 현명한 새 역사의 창조인가.

　인간은 역사의 주인이며, 정치는 때로 역사를 창조하는 힘을 발휘한다. 그래서 언어, 종교와 함께 인류의 3대 발명품에 정치를 넣는 것이리라. 남북 두 정상은 민족통일사에 새 역사를 창조했다. 그리고 이 사진집에 수록된 한 장, 한 장의 사진들은 그 현장을 생생히 증언하고 기록하는 역할을 할 것이다. 이 소중한 사진들을 통하여 민족의 평화통일이 어서 빨리 오기를 고대한다.

Foreword

Pictures Can Change History

by Novelist Jo Jung-rae

History is a vital part of our existence, detailing everything that has gone before us. However, history can take shape in our minds only when it is recorded. Therefore, recorded history is a novel concept available only to humankind that has words, the tool for recording.

However, humanity has another tool for recording-pictures. Sometimes, what pictures show is the despair of literature, arts, and music. Artists, writers, and musicians sometimes bemoan their lack of expressive skills when faced with the spectacular, marvelous manifestations of nature. But not photographers—their pictures can provide a duplication of what the eye sees.

However, pictures are not valued just in terms of their expressive capability. Sometimes, a single picture can change the course of history. One example is the picture of Jewish prisoners from WWII, men and women, young and old, stripped naked and being taken into the gas chamber. If it were not for this single picture, the world would never have shuddered so violently at the atrocities of the Nazis. Another example is the picture of layer after layer of corpses, stacked up like firewood. Had it not been for this picture, Japan would have been able to deny that the Nanjing Massacre ever happened. These are just a couple of examples of how a picture stands above, and even supersedes the ability of words to record history effectively.

The June 15 South-North Joint Declaration of 2000 was a turning point. The era of division changed course toward an era of unification. Building on that Declaration, the 2007 South-North Korean Summit was able to pave a highway that will take our nation to peaceful unification. The title of the declaration that came out of the summit was "Declaration on the Advancement of South-North Korean Relations, Peace and Prosperity." Unification has been a long-cherished national desire and earnest prayer that has yet to be answered. However, the two summits between the Koreas declared, in front of 70 million Koreans and the entire world, that the means to achieve unification will be peaceful and prosperous, not belligerent. What a prudent creation of a new history this declaration is!

Human beings are the main players on the stage of history, and politics sometimes demonstrates its power to create history. Therefore, there are people who include politics as one of the three major human creations, along with letters and religion. The two summits between South and North Korea have created a new chapter in the history of Korean unification. And each and every picture in this book is a clear representation of the scene where it takes place, constituting a solid record of the process. I hope that these priceless pictures will help bring peaceful unification to this divided nation sooner than anyone dreamed.

통일에 이르는 큰 강의 작은 징검다리

잘 찍은 사진 한 장, 특히 극적인 장면을 예리하게 포착한 보도사진에는 구구한 설명이 필요 없는 법이다. 현장이 주는 압도적 진실의 힘만으로도 보는 이들의 가슴을 충분히 전율시킬 수 있기 때문이다. 사진의 감동을 배가한답시고 어쭙잖게 붓방아를 놀리다가는 군더더기가 되기 십상이다.

1972년 6월 8일 AP통신의 베트남전쟁 프리랜서 종군기자인 후이 콩 우트가 찍은 '네이팜탄과 소녀'를 보자. 미군 전투기의 네이팜탄 투하로 불바다가 된 마을이 있다. 그 불길 속을 뚫고 온몸에 화상을 입은 채 알몸으로 울부짖으며 달려 나오던 아홉 살 소녀의 처절한 모습에서, 세계인들은 베트남전쟁의 야만성과 비극성을 새삼 절감했다. 더 이상 무슨 말이 필요했을까.

솔직히 처음 출판사의 제의를 받았을 때 적잖이 망설였다. 노무현 대통령과 김정일 국방위원장의 2007 남북정상회담을 담은 역사적인 장면에 '구구한 설명'을 붙여 봤자 췌언(贅言)밖에 더 되겠는가. 일개 서생의 시원찮은 필력으로 어찌 사진이 주는 진실의 위력을 담아낼 수 있을 것인가 하는 생각이 앞섰던 것이다.

그럼에도 불구하고 나서기로 결정했다. 이미 역사가 돼버린 장면, 장면을 제대로 풀어 간다면 그날의 감동과 민족사적 의의를 재현할 수도 있다는 생각이 들었다. 특히 '공식적인 주연(主演)'이었던 노 대통령이나 김 위원장 말고도 우리와 똑같이 웃고, 떠들고,

사랑하는 북녘의 보통 사람들을 보면서 욕구가 솟구쳤다. '비공식적인 조연(助演)'들의 모습을 짧으나마 반드시 문자로써 증거하고 싶었기 때문이다.

　사진에 대한 직접적 설명은 가급적 피하려고 했다. 보도를 통해 이미 알려진 것들이 대부분이었기 때문에, 사진이 주는 감동과 전체적인 맥락 따위를 포착하려고 나름대로 노력을 기울였다. 이를테면 '텍스트(text)'는 최소화하고 '컨텍스트(context)'는 최대화하려 했던 셈이다.

　이 책은, 지난 2000 남북정상회담에 이어 2007년 10월 2일부터 4일까지 평양에서 개최된 2007 남북정상회담 3일간의 영상 기록을 담은 것이다. 사실 이 책의 진정한 저자는 사진기자들이다. 장면 하나하나를 놓치지 않고 포착한 그들의 노고에 나는 그저 '구구한 설명'을 덧붙였을 뿐이다. 만일 이 책이 좋은 평가를 받는다면 그 공은 전적으로 책의 탄생을 계획하고, 지원하며, 흔쾌히 사진 촬영에 응했던 모든 사람들의 몫이다. 아무쪼록 이 사진집이 민족의 화해와 평화, 통일에 이르는 큰 강에 작은 징검다리가 되기를 바랄 뿐이다.

2007년 12월 서울 정동에서

손동우

A small steppingstone in a big river that will take us to national harmony

A well-taken photo, particularly a good news photo that smartly captures a dramatic scene, does not require any wordy caption. The power of the overwhelming truth that comes only from the actual scene can send chills through the hearts of the viewers. If one attempts to add a few words hoping to double the heart-touching effect of the photo, the words will most likely be redundant.

Take for example the photo titled 'Napalm Girl' taken on June 8, 1972 by Nick Ut, a freelancer battlefield reporter during the Vietnam War, working for AP. There was a village engulfed in flames after an American fighter dropped napalm. From the misery of the nine-year old girl, who was running out of the burning flames, naked in tears with her entire body burned by fire, the entire world could discover the atrocity and the misery of the Vietnam War. No further words were necessary.

Honestly, I hesitated not a little when I received the suggestion from the publishing company. What went through my mind was that, adding a few petty explanations to such historic pictures that captured the second South-North Summit between President Roh Moo-hyun and the leader of the North, Chairman Kim Jong Il, would be no more than adding redundancy, and how can the pen of a mere journalist put the power of truth coming from the photos into words.

Nevertheless, I ended up agreeing to it. I thought if I could adequately write down words to describe the scenes that have now become part of our history, I might be able to evoke the national significance and the heart-moving emotions all over again. In particular, I felt a desire burning up from inside, when I saw our beloved fellow ordinary citizens of the North, who smiled and talked just the same as any of us, not to mention President Roh and their leader Chairman Kim Jong Il. I wanted to provide evidence of the reality of those 'unofficial supporting players' from the North, if only in short sentences.

I wanted to stay away as much as possible from direct explanation of the scenes in the photos. Since they were already explained through news reports, I tried, on my own, to capture the underlying context and the way the photos touch our hearts. In other words, I tried to minimize the texts and maximize the context.

The South-North Summit meeting was held in Pyongyang for four days from October 2, 2007. It followed the one by former President Kim Dae-jung in 2000. In fact, the true authors of this book are the photo journalists. All I did was adding a few 'redundant explanations' to their efforts that captured every single moment of the historic event. If this book receives good feedback, the credit should go entirely to those who planned, supported and willingly agreed to having their photos taken. My sincere wish is that this photo catalogue will become a small steppingstone in a big river that will take us to national harmony, peace and even unification.

Son Dong-woo

2007 남북정상회담 2박 3일간의 주요 일정

(좌)청와대에서 대국민 담화 발표 후 출발
(우)분단 이래 최초로 군사분계선 도보 통과

(좌)평양 시내 카퍼레이드와 시민 환영 행사
(중)평양 4 · 25문화회관 광장에서 7년 만에 손을 맞잡은 남북 정상
(우)숙소인 백화원 영빈관에 도착

(위)만수대 의사당에서 김영남
최고인민회의 상임위원장과 면담
(아래)목란관에서 열린 공식 환영
만찬

(좌)백화원에서 수행원과 함께 조찬 간담회
(우)백화원 영빈관에서 총 2회, 4시간 3분에 걸쳐 남북정상회담

(좌)정상회담 2차 회의가 시작되기 직전 담소를 나누는 남북 정상
(우)대동강 능라도 5 · 1경기장에서 아리랑 공연 관람

인민문화궁전에서 답례 만찬 주최

(좌)남포 평화자동차 공장과 서해갑문 방문
(우)'남북관계 발전과 평화번영을 위한 선언'이 담긴 남북 정상 합의문 서명 및 교환

(좌)백화원 영빈관에서 열린 환송 오찬 참석
(우)평양 중앙식물원에서 남북정상회담 기념식수

(위 좌)조국통일 3대헌장 기념탑 광장에서 열린 공식 환송 행사 참석
(아래 좌)개성공단 방문
(우)도라산 남북출입사무소에서 환영 행사 참석

1부

만남

꿈결에도 불러 보고 싶었던 그 이름 "오마니"

● ● ●

'상봉' 의 사전적 의미는 '서로 만나는 것' 이지만 분단의 상처를 안고 있는 우리 민족에게 그 말은 처절한 비원이 서려 있는 것이기도 합니다. 1985년 9월 21일, 분단 이후 처음 이루어진 역사적인 이산가족 상봉에서 남녘의 어머니와 북녘의 아들이 울부짖으며 만나고 있습니다. "오마니, 어찌 이렇게 늙으셨어요." "아들아, 너도 늙어 가는구나." 두 모자의 모습이 애절하기만 합니다.

Mother, the Name You Called in Your Dreams

The meaning of "reunion" in the dictionary is to meet someone again, but for Koreans, who have been wounded by the division of the land, the word includes a sorrowful prayer as well. In this picture taken on September 21, 1985, a son from the North and his mother from the South have a tearful reunion for the first time since the nation was divided. "Mother, you have grown so old." "Son, you are getting old yourself." It pains us greatly to see the son and his mother.

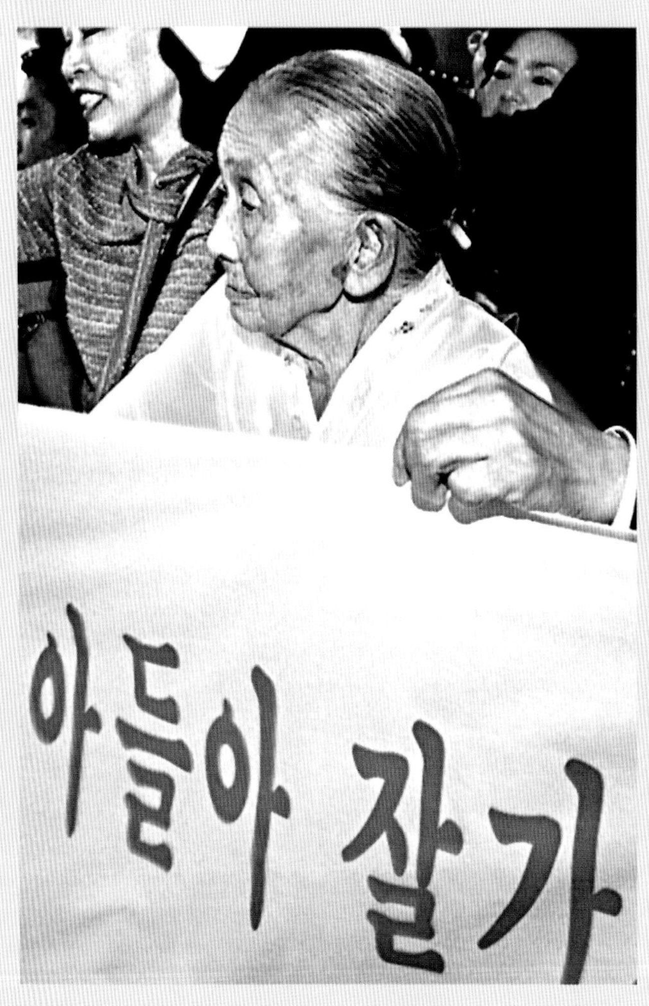
아들아 잘가

● ● ●

반세기 동안 쌓였던 태산 같은 그리움을 다 풀기에 상봉의 시간은 너무나 짧았습니다. 차라리 만나지 않았다면 이렇게 슬프지 않았을 것을. 현수막을 들고 북녘 아들을 보내는 남녘 노모는 이별의 아픔에 넋이 나간 듯 보입니다.

A Brief Meeting Making the Heart Race; Then a Long Heart-Wrenching Departure

The reunion was simply too short to relieve all the longings and yearnings that had accumulated for over a half century. They wouldn't have had to experience such sorrow if they had not met again. The aged mother from the South seems only distracted at the impending departure, as she holds a banner to see her son off to the North.

서러워라, 이별의 정표여

● ● ●

사랑하는 사람끼리는 그 사랑이 오래오래 이어지기를 기원하는 정표(情表)를 주고받습니다. 신혼부부나 연인들이 서로의 손가락에 끼워 주는 반지가 그 대표적인 예입니다. 재회의 기약 없이 헤어지는 이산가족들에게도 어찌 정표가 없을까요. 시계를 주고받는 이산가족의 주름진 손마디가 가늘게 떨리고 있습니다. 다시 만나려면 시곗바늘이 또 얼마나 더 돌아야 할는지.

What a Sorrowful Token of the Heart at the Time of Departing

Couples in love exchange tokens so that their love will be remembered for a long time. The most familiar example of such a token is the rings that young lovers exchange. Families who are divided in the South and North are also impelled to exchange tokens of love before departing with each other without any expectation of meeting again. The fingers of one of the separated family members tremble faintly, as she gives a watch as her token of love. How many times will the hands of the watch have to turn before they can meet again?

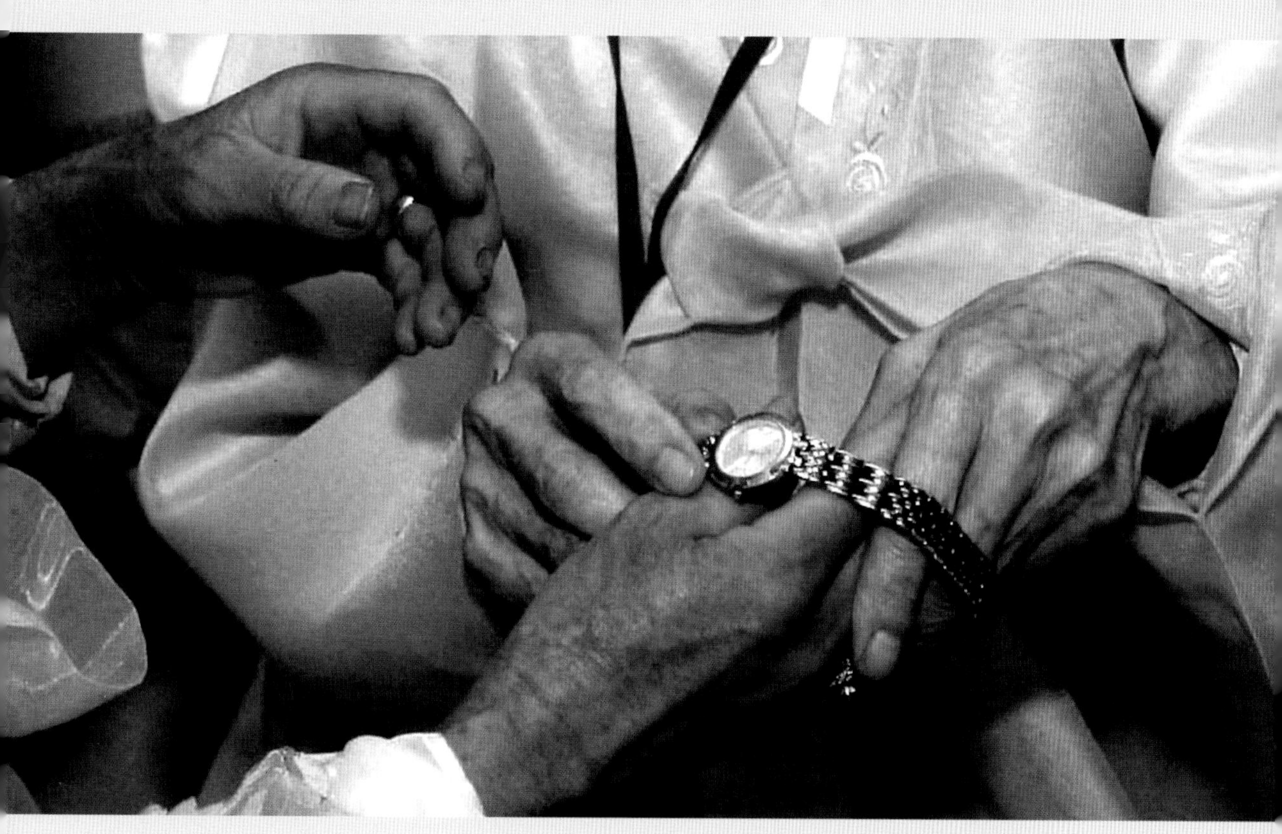

청와대의 천하대장군

• • •

옛날 마을 어귀에는 예외 없이 장승이 우뚝 서 있었습니다. '천하대장군(天下大將軍)'이나 '상원대장
군(上元大將軍)'으로 불리는 그들은 공동체의 안녕과 평화를 기원하는 임무를 맡았지요. 노무현 대통
령이 남북정상회담 출발에 앞서 청와대 본관 앞에서 대국민 담화를 발표하는 동안 울긋불긋한 조선
시대 군복을 입고 뒤편에 묵묵히 서 있는 국방부 전통의장대의 모습이 장승을 떠올리게 합니다. 노
무현 대통령의 출발 직전 세워진 이 '청와대 장승'이 회담의 성공을 간절히 염원하는 듯합니다.

Cheonha Daejanggun (Great General Under Heaven) at the Blue House

In ancient times in Korea, jangseung, or guardian spirit posts, could be found standing at the entrance
to every village without exception. Called Cheonha Daejanggun, these guardian spirit posts were
believed to expel evil and bring peace and security to the communities. There are two soldiers of the
Ministry of National Defense (MND) Honor Guard, dressed in traditional military uniforms from the
Joseon Kingdom (1392-1910), standing behind President Roh Moo-hyun as he delivers his speech to
the nation in front of Cheong Wa Dae, the presidential office/residence, before leaving for the South-
North Korean Summit. They remind us of jangseung. Having taken up their positions right before
President Roh's departure for the summit, these two "Jangseung of Cheong Wa Dae" seem to be
praying earnestly for the success of the summit.

● ● ●

태극기와 대통령 문장을 단 최첨단 벤츠가 평양으로 달릴 준비를 하고 있습니다. 한국인에게 벤츠로 잘 알려진 독일 메르세데스 벤츠 승용차는 갖가지 방호 기능과 함께 최첨단 기능을 갖춰, 세계 여러 나라 정상들의 전용차로 성가를 떨치고 있습니다. 벤츠와 그 앞에서 전통 관복을 입고 전통 의례를 행하는 국방부 전통의장대의 모습이 절묘한 조화를 이룹니다.

Harmony of Tradition and Technology

The latest model Benz with the presidential emblem and Taegeuk-gi (the national flag) is getting ready for the trip to the North Korean capital of Pyongyang. This German-made Mercedes Benz, the ultimate symbol of luxury cars, has the reputation of being the designated car for summits around the world, with their many protective safety features built with the latest technology. The MND Honor Guards dressed in traditional military uniforms and performing a time-honored ceremony create a striking image in contrast to the Benz that stands in front of them.

큰일을 하는 사람만큼 알리는 사람도 바쁘다

● ● ●

남북정상회담과 같은 중대한 일을 할 때는 이 일을 주도하여 수행하는 사람도 분주하지만, 그것을
국민들에게 알리는 기자들도 눈코 뜰 새가 없습니다. 노무현 대통령이 관저를 출발하기 직전 청와대
대정원에 진을 치고 있는 방송사 차량과 취재진들의 분주한 발걸음이 새삼 회담의 중요성과 의미를
환기시켜 줍니다.

The Reporters Are As Busy As the Main Players

When there is a major event like the South-North Korean Summit, reporters—who are responsible for
relaying details of the event to the people—are no less busy than those who are on center stage.
Broadcast vehicles and quick-moving reporters camp inside Cheong Wa Dae as President Roh is about
to leave, reminding us once again how important and significant the summit talks are.

● ● ●

노무현 대통령이 북으로 출발하기 직전 각료들과 청와대 참모들이 좌우로 도열해 있습니다. 가방을 들고 있는 수행원들의 표정에서 설렘과 긴장감이 읽혀집니다. 무릇 집을 나서 먼 길을 떠날 때면 가슴 벅찬 설렘과 야릇한 감정이 교차하는 법입니다. 하물며 역사적인 정상회담을 위해 북으로 가는 사람들의 마음이야 더했으면 더했지 덜하지 않으리라 봅니다.

Anticipation of the Journey
The presidential staff line up on either side of President Roh Moo-hyun, as he addresses the nation before leaving for the North. We can see the nervousness and excitement in the faces of the accompanying staff, who are carrying briefcases. It is natural to feel a sense of adventure and anticipation before leaving on a long journey, but we can assume that this is especially true for those who are going to the North to participate in a historic summit.

● ● ●

노무현 대통령이 평양으로 향하기 직전 서울 도심은 축제 분위기를 한껏 돋우는 표정이었습니다. 환송 나온 시민들의 기대 어린 얼굴, 곳곳에 내걸린 태극기가 정상회담에 대한 온 국민의 바람을 대변하는 듯합니다. 환송 시민들을 안내하기 위해 줄지어 서 있는 전의경들의 모습이 군사독재 정권 시절 진압을 위해 도열해 있곤 하던 전의경들과 대비돼 격세지감을 느끼게 합니다.

Taegeuk-gi (national flags), Citizens, and Police—All Coming Together

The city of Seoul was in a festive mood right before President Roh Moo-hyun left for Pyongyang. The looks on the faces of citizens who came out on the street to see him off and the flags flying on many street corners seem to be a manifestation of what the entire nation is expecting from this summit. The police, neatly lining the street to guide well-wishers, are in sharp contrast to those of the past military-influenced administrations, who were mobilized to protect presidents from protesters. They are from two worlds, poles apart, indeed.

당신과 함께 갑니
참여정부 평가포럼

마음은 풍선에 싣고, 정성은 현수막에 담아

● ● ●

"우리들 마음이 당신과 함께 갑니다."
노무현 대통령 일행을 환송하기 위해 정부중앙청사 연도에 모인 시민들이 형형색색의 풍선과 한반도기, 현수막을 들고 상기된 표정을 짓고 있습니다. 시민들이 하늘로 날려 보낸 풍선 하나하나가 한반도 전역을 굽어보고, 이들의 하나 된 마음이 평양까지 노무현 대통령과 동행해서 회담의 성공과 민족의 화해에 크게 기여하리라 믿습니다.

Hearts in Balloons, Sincerity on the Banner

"Our hearts are going with you." Citizens lining the street near the Central Government Complex to see President Roh and his delegation off are excited, as they hold a rainbow of colored balloons and Unification Flags (a blue peninsula on a white background) behind a large banner. Each balloon the citizens released into the sky will float over the Korean Peninsula symbolizing their united hearts following President Roh Moo-hyun all the way to Pyongyang and carrying wishes for national harmony and a successful summit.

● ● ●

이른 아침부터 서울 도심 곳곳에는 태극기가 내걸렸습니다. 청와대에서 정부중앙청사에 이르는 큰길에는 아무것도 보이지 않다가 이윽고 불빛이 번쩍거렸습니다. 노무현 대통령 일행을 태운 차량과 경찰 호위 차량들이었습니다. 시민들의 박수 소리와 힘차게 흔들리는 태극기, 하늘로 둥둥 떠올라 가는 풍선… 자, 이제 출발입니다.

Taegeuk-gi after Taegeuk-gi Flying on the Street

Beginning early in the morning, the Taegeuk-gi started to appear in every nook and cranny in the city of Seoul. The major road that stretches between the Cheong Wa Dae and the Government Complex was completely empty, until lights started to glitter in the distance—lights from the vehicles carrying President Roh and his group and the police escort vehicles. Then along with the thunderous applause of the citizens came a wave of national flags and balloons rising into the sky⋯ Now, the journey had begun.

● ● ●

남북정상회담을 맞아 임진강 통일대교 철조망에는 민족의 염원을 담은 갖가지 사연이 나붙었습니다. 시민들은 회담의 성공을 축원하면서, 남과 북이 오래된 불신을 씻고 화해와 평화로 나아가기를 기원했습니다. 그리하여 끊어진 우리 국토와 민족의 마음이 마침내 하나로 합쳐지기를 빌고, 또 빌었습니다.

What Wishes and Prayers Could These Notes Hold?
Personal notes—that carry the wishes of the nation—began to appear on the barbed wire along the Unification Bridge at the Imjingang (river) as the South-North Korean Summit approached. Citizens were praying for success of the summit. They wished for the South and the North to move beyond a long era of distrust and instead begin the march toward harmony and peace, so that the divided land and hearts of the people would finally be united as one.

북한강 맑은 물은 한반도 허리의 경계선을 뚫는다

● ● ●

지뢰 매설 지역임을 알리는 표지판과 철조망, 경계 근무를 서고 있는 국군 병사 등 강원도 중동부 전
선 최전방인 북한강 상류 지역의 풍경이 새삼 우리 국토가 분단돼 있음을 일깨워 줍니다. 그러나 밑
바닥이 훤히 보이는 맑은 강물은 그것을 아는지 모르는지 그저 유유하게 흘러만 갑니다.

The Clear Waters of Bukhan-gang Runs Through the Dividing Line of the Korean Peninsula
The scene at the upper reaches of the Bukhan-gang (river), the foremost front line in the central
eastern part of Gangwon-do (province) reminds us that Korea is a divided nation. There we can see
soldiers guarding the country, barbed wire and a sign that indicates the area is a minefield. But the
clear water flowing so peacefully is unaware of the harsh reality.

지 뢰
MINE

영화와 현실은 달라야 한다

● ● ●

영화 〈공동경비구역 JSA〉에서 남북한 병사들의 이데올로기를 초월한 우정은, 그로 인한 비극적 결말 때문에 더욱 관객들의 가슴을 울렸습니다. 판문점 공동경비구역. 늘 팽팽한 긴장감이 감도는 곳. 그러나 이곳에서도 젊은 청년들은 서로에 대한 우정을 키워 가고 있을지 모릅니다. 하지만 현실은 결코 영화처럼 비극으로 끝나선 안 됩니다.

Reality Is Different From the Movies

The movie Joint Security Area touched the hearts of viewers with a story of friendship between the soldiers of the South and the North transcending ideology, which ended with miserable consequences. Perhaps young soldiers at the Joint Security Area near Panmunjeom, where tensions remain high the year round, are building friendships. But the reality should not be allowed to end in misery, as it did in the movie.

하늘 높이 나는 새들에게는 남북이 없다

● ● ●

휴전선, 군사분계선, 북방한계선 등 한반도를 둘로 갈라놓는 갖가지 경계선도 창공을 비상하는 이 자유로운 존재들에게는 아무런 제약을 가하지 못합니다. 비무장지대 부근에 서식하는 철새들이 떼를 지어 군사시설 위를 날고 있습니다.

Birds in the Sky Do Not Recognize South or North

There are many dividing lines on the Korean Peninsula, such as the Demilitarized Zone, the Military Demarcation Line and the Northern Limit Line, but those divisions do not restrict the birds high in the sky. A migrating flock is flying over a military facility near the Demilitarized Zone.

파주시 입니다
Welcome to Paju
후방10m
파주시
Paju

2007년 10월 2일 09시 05분!

●●●

우리 역사에서 이 순간은 아마도 오래오래 기억될 것입니다. 남북이 분단된 이래 처음으로 걸어서 군사분계선을 통과했고, 그 주인공이 바로 대한민국 대통령이었기 때문입니다. 노무현 대통령의 첫 걸음으로 빗장이 열린 노란색 군사분계선은 앞으로 수많은 사람들의 분주한 발걸음으로 점점 색깔이 벗겨지고 희미해지다 마침내 그 모습을 감출 것입니다. 그날이, 그 벅찬 순간이 머지않아 반드시 오리라는 것을 역사는 알고 있습니다.

October 2, 2007, 09:05!

This moment will be remembered in history for a long time. For the first time since the land was divided into South and North, the Military Demarcation Line (MDL) has been crossed on foot, and the one who took this historic step is none other than the President of the Republic of Korea. Now that the gate to the MDL has been unlocked, many other feet will follow, until the paint over the line is worn away and finally disappears completely. History will record that day, and the moment will surely come before long.

지금부터는 저희가 모시겠습니다

• • •

경계선이란 그것이 양분하고 있는 두 개체의 성격을 서로 다르게, 때로는 대립적으로 만듭니다. 노
란색 페인트로 칠한 가느다란 선에 불과한 군사분계선도 한반도를 대한민국과 조선민주주의인민공
화국이란 두 개의 서로 다른 체제로 나눠 놓고 있습니다. 노무현 대통령이 군사분계선을 넘자 기다
리고 있던 북한 통일전선부 최승철 부부장이 안내하고 있습니다.

From This Moment On, We Are At Your Service
A dividing line can make the people on either side go their different ways, and sometimes those ways
are antagonistic. The Military Demarcation Line may be just an invisible line painted yellow for this
occasion, but it has been dividing the Korean Peninsula into two different systems—the Republic of
Korea and the Democratic Peoples' Republic of Korea. As President Roh Moo-hyun crosses the MDL,
Choe Sung Chol, deputy director of the United Front Department, who has been waiting for his arrival,
steps forward to greet him.

환
2007 남북정상회담 평화와 번영의 길
통일의 관문
대한민국

오늘, 농악이 없을 수 없다

● ● ●

오늘같이 좋은 날, 화해와 평화를 위해 달려가는 날, 어찌 신명나는 놀이 한마당이 없겠습니까? 농악대의 흥겨운 몸짓이 축제 분위기를 한껏 살리고 있습니다. 풍요로운 수확을 기원하고, 알찬 결실을 맺었을 때 하늘에 감사하는 농악대의 마음이 남북정상회담의 성공을 기원하는 바로 그 마음일 것입니다.

Today Is a Day for a Farmers Dance

On a wonderful day like today, when we are racing towards national peace and harmony, we cannot do without some excitement. The invigorating movements of the farmers' band are firing up the already festive mood. The traditional purpose of a performance by a farmers' band was to wish for a bountiful harvest and to thank Heaven for the successful outcome. Here the performance expresses a wish for the success of the South-North Korean Summit.

길은 열려 있어야 길이다

• • •

무릇 길은 항상 열려 있어야 하고, 그 열린 길 위를 많은 사람들이 다닐 수 있어야 합니다. 길이 길인 까닭은 사람과 사람 사이를 이어 주고, 사람이 사람에게 다가갈 수 있는 소통의 공간이기 때문입니다. 통일대교를 떠나 북쪽으로 향하는 노무현 대통령 일행의 뒤편으로 '평화를 다지는 길, 번영으로 가는 길'이라는 비석이 보입니다. 아마도 이번 정상회담을 준비하면서, 노무현 대통령이 이루고자 하는 모든 것을 함축적으로 표현한 것이겠지요.

A Path Becomes a Road When It Is Used Often

A path is meant to stay open, so that many people can walk along it. A path becomes a road when it connects people and allows them to reach out to each other. As President Roh Moo-hyun heads to the North toward Unification Bridge, he passes a stone monument with an inscription he wrote, "A Road to Solidify Peace, A Road to Take Us to Prosperity." The monument expresses what the President wished to achieve as he prepared for the historic occasion.

평화를 다지는 길
번영으로 가는 길
2007. 10. 2.
대한민국 대통령 노무현
2007 남북정상회담

경의선을 타고 신의주 여행을 갈수 있기를 바라며
"2007남북정상회담의 성공적 개최를 기원합니다."
민주평화통일자문회의 자문위원 일동

경의선 타고 신의주 갈 수 있다면

● ● ●

보통 사람들이 남북 화해나 평화, 나아가 통일에 대해 품고 있는 생각은 그다지 거창하거나 복잡하지 않습니다. 가고 싶은 곳이 떠오르면 언제든지 갈 수 있고, 보고 싶은 사람이 생각나면 아무 때라도 만날 수 있으면 되는 것입니다. 통일대교 남단에 나붙은 '경의선을 타고 신의주 여행을 갈 수 있기를 바라며'라는 글귀가 쓰인 현수막에 그 같은 소박한 염원이 잘 담겨 있습니다.

If Only We Could Reach Sinuiju Via the Seoul-Sinuiju Railroad Line

What ordinary people expect from the South-North reconciliation, peace, or even eventual unification is not necessarily grand or complex. For the most part, it would be enough if they were free to go where they wished to go, or meet someone whom they suddenly missed and wished to see. The large banner that is posted on the southern section of Unification Bridge, which reads "We wish we could travel to Sinuiju via the Seoul-Sinuiju Railroad Line," clearly articulates the simple and basic wishes of ordinary people.

얼마 남지 않은 평양 길, 그러나 앞으로 계속 나아가야 할 길

● ● ●

요즘 자동차로 달려 한 시간 남짓 하는 거리라면 그야말로 지척인 셈입니다. 노무현 대통령 일행을 태운 방북 행렬 옆으로 '평양 92km'란 이정표가 보입니다. 남과 북의 물리적 거리가 아주 가깝다는 것, 그리고 아직도 더 좁혀야 할 정서적 거리가 남아 있다는 것을 동시에 보여 주는 듯합니다. 북측 도로를 달리는 차들은 남측에서 생산된 것들이며, 운전도 남측 사람들이 맡았습니다. 남과 북의 계속적인 만남은 그 가까운 거리마저 더욱 좁혀줄 것입니다.

The Road to Pyongyang Is Not Long, And We Must Follow It To the End
These days, an hour's trip by car is considered a short distance. A road sign that says "Pyongyang, 92 km" is shown next to President Roh Moo-hyun's motorcade on its way to North Korea. The sign seems to be telling us that the physical distance between the South and the North is very short, but the emotional distance is still long. What is important here is that South Korean vehicles are cruising along the North Korean highway. Continuous meetings between the South and North will help close the gap between the two sides.

평 양
92 km
05ᄑ8318
5206729
11ᄂ5193

휴게소에서도 부동자세(?)

● ● ●

남북정상회담이라는 국가적 대사의 무게감 때문이었을까요? 수곡휴게소를 방문한 노무현 대통령과
수행원들이 근엄하게 부동자세를 취하고 있는 모습이 어딘지 이채롭습니다. 큰일을 앞두고 사진 등
을 찍을 때면 곧잘 그러는 보통 사람들과 대통령 일행 또한 크게 다르지 않음을 보여 주는 장면입니
다. 그래도 휴게소인데 좀 더 편안하고 자연스러운 모습을 보였으면 좋았을 것을.

Standing at Attention Even at a Rest Stop
President Roh Moo-hyun and his delegation take a formal photo during their stop at the Sugok Rest
Stop, creating an odd impression. Like ordinary people having their picture taken on an important
occasion, the Korean delegation, including the President, looks somewhat stiff. It would have been
nicer if they could have relaxed at the rest stop.

휴게소의 백두산 호랑이

● ● ●

저 늠름한 자태를 자랑하는 백두산 호랑이도 남북정상회담이 열리는 것을 반기는 것일까요? 수곡휴
게소에 들른 노무현 대통령 일행이 실내에 전시된 호랑이 그림과 북녘의 아름다운 풍광을 묘사한 산
수도 등을 감상하고 있습니다. 호랑이의 형형한 눈매는 화해와 평화통일을 향한 남북한 구성원 모두
의 소중한 노력들을 하나도 놓치지 않고 앞으로도 계속 지켜볼 것입니다.

Tiger of Baekdusan on Display at a Rest Stop
Is that imposing tiger of the Baekdusan (mountain) in the background also welcoming the South-North
Summit? During their short visit to the Sugok Rest Stop, President Roh Moo-hyun and his delegation
view paintings of tigers and landscapes of the beautiful scenery of the North. The glowing eyes of the
tiger will keep watch over them all, without missing a single moment of the hard work of the South
and North Korean officials to achieve national harmony and peaceful unification.

21세기의 태양 김정일장군 만세 !

김일성 주석도 환영 대열에 동참했는가?

● ● ●

북한의 대표적인 풍경 가운데 하나가 바로 곳곳에 서 있는 김일성 주석의 동상입니다. 그가 사망한
지 벌써 13년이 지났지만 이른바 그의 '유훈통치'는 아직도 효력을 발휘하고 있다는 느낌이 듭니다.
노무현 대통령을 맞은 평양 시민들의 환영 대열 뒤편에 김일성 주석의 동상이 보입니다. 오른팔을
앞으로 쭉 내민 특유의 모습이 마치 시민들과 함께 노무현 대통령의 평양 방문을 반기는 듯합니다.

Is the Late Leader Kim Il-sung Also Taking Part in the Welcome?

One of the most iconic scenes of North Korea are the statues of the late leader Kim Il-sung, which
stand in various places throughout the land. He's been dead for over 13 years now, but his so-called
"instructions of the departed" seem to be still in effect even today. One of his statues is seen in this
photo, behind a crowd of Pyongyang citizens greeting President Roh Moo-hyun. His outstretched arm
seems to be welcoming President Roh Moo-hyun to Pyongyang, along with the citizens.

● ● ●

경축일에는 역시 고적대의 연주가 있어야 흥이 나는 법입니다. 원래 고적대(鼓笛隊)는 문자 그대로 북과 피리로만 이뤄진 악대를 뜻하지만 요즈음은 그 밖의 다른 악기들도 포함돼 있습니다. 인민문화 궁전 앞의 북소리와 피리소리, 남녘 대통령을 맞아 높이 높이 울려 퍼집니다.

Marching Band Best Suits the Welcoming Ceremony

The performance of a marching band is what it takes to bring excitement to a celebration. In the traditional sense, a marching band consisted of drums and fifes, but nowadays, it includes many other types of musical instruments. The sound of the band rises high into the air in front of the People's Palace of Culture to welcome the President from the South.

아름다운 한복, 수줍은 미소

● ● ●

북한 여성들이 한복을 곱게 차려입은 모습을 볼 때마다, 지금 남녘에서는 보기 어려운 단아한 전통 미인을 만나는 듯한 느낌을 갖게 됩니다. 공식 환영 장소인 인민문화궁전에 도착한 노무현 대통령 내외가 젊은 여성 두 명에게서 꽃다발을 건네받은 뒤 악수를 나누고 있습니다. 다소곳이 고개를 숙인 채 오른손으로는 노무현 대통령의 손을 잡고 왼손은 노무현 대통령의 손등에 가볍게 대고 있는 여성의 모습이 아름답습니다.

Beautiful Hanbok, Bashful Smiles

Women from the North, beautifully dressed in traditional Korean costumes, or Hanbok, make people wonder if they have traveled back in time to meet elegant ladies of the past—a rarity these days in the South. President Roh Moo-hyun and the First Lady are shaking hands with two young ladies who have just presented them with bouquets upon their arrival at the People's Palace of Culture, where the official welcoming ceremony is to take place.

일에서 제시된 전투적과업을 철

'전투적 환영'은 뜨거운 환영이다

● ● ●

평양 시내 카퍼레이드를 벌이는 노무현 대통령과 김영남 최고인민회의 상임위원장의 표정이 재미있습니다. 노무현 대통령은 시민들의 뜨거운 환영에 감격스러운 듯한 표정을 짓고 있고, 김영남 위원장은 '가장 귀한 손님'을 맞아 흐뭇한 미소를 띠고 있습니다. 일제히 북을 치며 환영하는 학생들의 모습 뒤에 '전투적 과업을 철저히 관철하자'는 '전투적'인 현수막이 환영 분위기와 묘하게 조화를 이룹니다.

A "Combative Welcome" Is a Passionate Welcome

President Roh Moo-hyun and Kim Young-nam, the Chairman of North Korea's Supreme People's Assembly, show interesting facial expressions as they pass down a street in Pyongyang in an open car. President Roh Moo-hyun appears touched at such an enthusiastic welcome by the citizens, while Chairman Kim Young-nam is pleased to greet one of the most important guestss. The banner behind the students who are beating drums to welcome the President and his group reads "enthusiastically carrying out our combative duties," creating a peculiar harmony with the welcoming mood.

환영은 아무래도 뜨거운 것이 좋다

● ● ●

북한 동포들이 손님을 맞아 환영하는 모습은 뜨겁고 힘차다는 느낌을 줍니다. 남녘 일각에서는 이를 자연스럽지 않다고 비판하기도 하지만, 북한 특유의 의전 방식을 고려한다면 나쁘게 볼 일만도 아닙니다. 특히 환영 현장의 열띤 분위기는 환영하는 사람이나 환영받는 사람 모두를 한껏 들뜨게 한다는 점에서 그렇습니다.

When Celebrating, the More Enthusiastic the Better

The way that residents of the North welcome guests creates an air of passion and power. Some from the South criticize it for being unnatural. However, we cannot really do that, considering the unique protocol in the North. It is particularly so when the passionate atmosphere of the welcoming ceremony is fired up with excitement both for those who are welcoming the guests and for those who are being welcomed.

● ● ●

노무현 대통령 행렬이 개성 시내를 지나갈 때 나들이를 나온 듯한 가족 단위의 시민들이 순간적으로
‘환영 모드’로 전환하는 모습입니다. 어린 소녀는 두 손을 흔들며 깡충깡충 뛰고, 여성들은 오른손을
자연스럽게 흔드는데, 가장인 듯한 남성은 멀뚱하게 담배만 피우고 있는 모습이 너무나 자연스러워
더욱 정겹기만 합니다.

A Spontaneous Welcome is Heartwarming

As the parade of President Roh Moo-hyun and the South Korean delegation passes through the city of
Gaeseong, even those citizens who just happen to be on the street for personal reasons spontaneously
join the welcoming crowd. The way the child is bouncing up and down and waving both arms and the
woman is casually waving, while the man, perhaps the head of the family, smokes a cigarette, looks
so natural that it is heartwarming.

데이트가 더 중요하다

● ● ●

그날 평양의 분위기가 환영 일색만은 아니었습니다. 노무현 대통령이 카퍼레이드를 벌이고 있는 동안 양장으로 곱게 차려입은 젊은 여성이 바쁘게 걸음을 옮기고 있습니다. 때마침 동년배로 보이는 여성 교통안내원이 부러운 듯 이 광경을 물끄러미 바라보고 있습니다. 남녀 대통령이 와도 관계없이 '데이트'(데이트가 아닐 수도 있지만) 하러 가는 젊은 여성, 이를 부러워하는 또 다른 여성의 모습이 평양이 서울이나 부산, 대구나 광주와 똑같이 사람 사는 곳임을 새삼 일깨워 줍니다.

Dating is More Important

A welcoming mood was not the only mood in Pyongyang that day. While President Roh Moo-hyun was taking part in a parade, a young lady, beautifully dressed in western style, was rushing somewhere. A female traffic officer, who appears to be of a similar age, stares at her, seemingly with envious eyes. From the sight of the young woman, whose only concern for the moment is to get where she's going in spite of the visiting President from the South and the officer, who is envious of her, we realize that Pyongyang is not much different from Seoul, Busan, Daegu, or Gwangju—it is a place where people live normal lives.

일은 즐겁다

● ● ●

초등학교 시절 장학사가 온다며 운동장의 사금파리를 줍고, 반들반들하도록 바닥에 윤을 냈던 즐겁지 않은 기억을 가진 이들이 적지 않을 것입니다. 설마 남녘의 대통령이 온다고 시민들이 도로 정비 작업에 동원됐을까요? 리어카에 삽을 싣고 일터로 떠나는 여성들의 표정이 즐겁기만 합니다.

Work Is Fun

Many of us still remember, with displeasure, the times during our elementary school days when the president of the local Board of Education was visiting the school, and we were sent out to pick up litter like broken glass or to mop the classroom floor until it shone. The citizens in this picture couldn't have been driven out to repair the road just because the President of the South was coming, could they? The women look happy as they make their way to work with shovels in their handcart.

신나는 나들이

● ● ●

젊은 아빠는 아기 용품 가방을 들었습니다. 세련된 차림의 젊은 엄마는 따가운 햇살에 대비해 양산을 들고 있습니다. 엄마 품에 안긴 아기는 예쁜 모자까지 쓰고 바깥 풍경이 신기한 듯 주위를 두리번거립니다. 신세대 가족의 나들이 풍경은 남이나 북이나 너무 똑같습니다.

Enjoyable Outing

A young couple with a baby scurries along a street in Pyongyang. The young dad is carrying the baby paraphernalia and the stylishly dressed young wife is holding a parasol. The baby wearing a pretty hat in the mother's arms is looking around as if everything is interesting. The scene of a family outing is pretty much the same in the South and the North.

걷는 시간도 아깝다

● ● ●

많은 지식을 쌓으려면 걷는 시간도 아껴야 합니다. 개성의 여학생들이 책을 보며 시내를 걷고 있습니다. 시험이 다가와 교과서나 참고서를 보는 것이겠지요. 아니면 사춘기 소녀들이 빠져들 만한 순정 연애 소설이거나.

Study Time Is Precious, Even While Walking

You can build knowledge, even while walking. Two female students in Gaeseong are reading books while walking down the street. They might be reading a textbook in preparation for an upcoming test. Or, they could be reading love stories that fascinate them.

평양에도 콩나물 버스(?)

● ● ●

콩나물 버스를 타는 것은 누구에게나 불편합니다. 하지만 사람은 역시 사람 속에 있어야 한다는 사실을 새삼 느끼게 만들기도 하지요. 서울, 부산에만 콩나물시루 같은 버스가 있는 줄 알았더니 평양에도 있었습니다. 역시 평양은 대도시인 모양입니다. 남북정상회담 수행 취재기자들이 카메라를 들이대자 버스에 타고 있던 시민들이 일제히 창밖을 바라보며 반색하고 있습니다.

People Packed Like Sardines in Buses, Even in Pyongyang?

Riding on a bus packed like sardines is uncomfortable. Yet, it sometimes makes us realize that people need to be with other people to feel alive. If you thought people were packed like sardines in buses only in Seoul or Busan, think again—the same bus is running in Pyongyang. Pyongyang is a metropolis after all. When the reporters covering the South-North Korean Summit pointed their cameras at them, the citizens stared back from behind the windows of the bus.

만남, 악수, 그리고 반가운 인사

● ● ●

만남은 처음이 가장 설레게 마련이지만 정작 신뢰와 애정이 쌓이려면 자주, 격의 없이 만나야 하는 법입니다. 남북 정상이 만나는 이 광경은 이미 우리에게 익숙합니다. 노무현 대통령이 서 있는 자리에 2000년 6월 김대중 전 대통령이 있었기 때문입니다. 당시의 벅찬 감동과 희열은 이제는 절제와 차분함으로 바뀌었습니다. 아마도 세 번째, 네 번째 정상회담은 더욱 안정되고 내실을 기하는 방향으로 전개될 것이며, 다섯 번째, 여섯 번째는 더욱 그러할 것입니다.

Meet, Shake Hands, and Exchange Greetings

A meeting is most thrilling in the first stage, but what it takes to build trust and affection is frequent, openhearted meetings. We are now familiar with the scene of the two South-North summits. That is because where President Roh Moo-hyun is standing now in this picture former President Kim Dae-jung stood in June 2000. The thrill and explosive emotion we felt back then has now somewhat dissipated. Perhaps, the third and fourth summits will be even more subdued and geared to building further substantial achievements. And so will all the rest.

그날은 말이 필요 없었다

● ● ●

2000년 6월 13일 〈경향신문〉은 1면을 전면 사진 1장만으로 채웠습니다. 김대중 전 대통령과 김정일 국방위원장의 감격적인 만남에 '구구한 설명'이 필요 없었기 때문입니다. 한국 언론사를 통틀어 신문 한 면에 단 한 자도 넣지 않고 광고도 싣지 않은 채 사진만 게재한 것은 그때가 처음이었습니다. 남북한 정상이 처음으로 두 손을 맞잡은 이 순간은 이미 민족 화해의 상징적 장면으로 굳어져 있습니다.

Words Were Not Necessary That Day

The front page of the Kyunghyang Daily News on June 13, 2000 was filled with a single full-page photo. No word of explanation was necessary for the dramatic meeting of former President Kim Dae-jung and the leader from the North, Chairman Kim Jong Il. In the history of Korean journalism, it was the first time that a page of a newspaper was filled with a single photo, without any word or advertisement. The moment when the leaders of the South and the North clasped each other's hands for the first time is already solidified as a symbol of national reconciliation.

● ● ●

'남조선'의 국군통수권자인 노무현 대통령을 맞아 적어도 겉으로는 최대의 경의를 표해야 하는 인민
군 병사는 어떤 느낌을 갖게 될까요? 아마도 혼란스러움과 어색함 따위가 적지 않을 것입니다. 조만
간 김정일 국방위원장이 남쪽으로 내려와 국군 사열을 할 때 우리 젊은 병사들이 느끼는 바도 크게
다르지 않을 것입니다. 그러나 그 같은 혼란은 시간의 흐름에 따라 자연스러움으로 바뀔 것이고, 서
로의 가슴속에 쌓였던 불신의 벽도 허물어질 것입니다.

An Encounter Between the Southern Commander-in-Chief and the Korean People's Army

One can only wonder what was going through the hearts of the soldiers of the North's People's Army, who needed to show the highest respect to the Commander-in-Chief from the South. Perhaps, they would have mixed feelings. When and if Kim Jong II, the Chairman of the National Defense Commission, comes to the South and inspects the honor guard, what would go through the hearts of our soldiers would not be much different. But such confusion will wane with the passing of time and instead will develop into a more natural response, and the wall of distrust will eventually break down.

● ● ●

한국전쟁 이후 남북한은 오랫동안 군사적 대결과 긴장 상태를 지속해 왔습니다. 그것의 극단적인 형태가 바로 1968년 북한 124군 부대 요원들의 '청와대 습격 사건'이었습니다. 이들은 박정희 전 대통령의 목숨을 노렸습니다. 인민군 의장대를 사열하는 김대중 전 대통령. 그러나 인민군 병사들의 총구(銃口)는 하늘로 향해 있습니다. '남조선 대통령'을 위협하는 것이 아니라 최대의 경의를 표하는 것이기 때문입니다.

The President of the Republic of Korea and the Guns of the People′s Army

Since the Korean War armistice, inter-Korean ties have remained in a state of tension and confrontation. The most dramatic manifestation of the situation was the commando attack on Cheong Wa Dae in 1968 by infiltrators from North Korean Special Unit 124. They were targeting then President Park Chung Hee. In this picture, former President Kim Dae-jung is inspecting the Honor Guard of the North's People's Army. But the guns of the soldiers are directed toward the sky. That is because they wish to show their highest respect to the President of the South and demonstrate that they are not a threat to him.

● ● ●

김대중 전 대통령과 김정일 국방위원장의 회담이 더욱 원활하게 진행된 이유 중 하나는 두 사람의 나이 차이가 상당했기 때문이라고 합니다. 김 전 대통령의 '노령' 이 '인륜도덕' 을 중시하는 김정일 국방위원장의 스타일과 맞아떨어졌다는 것입니다. 음식을 앞에 놓고 김정일 국방위원장의 말을 듣고 있는 김대중 전 대통령의 표정이 진지하고 따뜻합니다.

Does the Age Difference of the Leaders Really Matter?

According to many people, one of the reasons the summit between former President Kim Dae-jung and the Chairman of the National Defense Commission Kim Jong Il was successful was because the two had a significant age gap. They said the fact that the former South Korean President was an elderly man was a significant advantage when meeting the Chairman of the National Defense Commission, who places great value on traditional ethics. Former President Kim Dae-jung is listening attentively to Chairman Kim Jong Il during dinner.

'졸병'은 '자상한 고참'이 늘 고맙기만 하다

● ● ●

군대를 다녀온 경험이 있는 이들은 잘 알고 있습니다. 유격훈련이나 각개전투보다는 줄 서고 발맞추는 제식훈련이 더 힘들다는 것을. 공식 환영 행사를 위해 4·25문화회관 광장에 나온 인민군 병사들의 휴식 시간 광경이 정겹습니다. '고참'이 '졸병'의 모자를 고쳐 주자 '졸병'은 '고참'의 자상함에 새삼 고마움을 느끼는 듯 눈을 지그시 감고 있습니다.

Junior Soldiers Are Always Appreciative of Considerate Seniors
Those who have served in the army are well aware of this; the drill training that teaches synchronization is more difficult than battle training. This scene of soldiers from the North Korean People's Army who were waiting to be called up to the plaza in front of the April 25 Hall of Culture for the official welcoming ceremony is heart-warming to watch. As one senior soldier fixes the hat of his junior, he closes his eyes, as if savoring the thoughtfulness of his superior.

〈태백산맥〉과 김정일 국방위원장

● ● ●

노무현 대통령과 함께 방북한 특별 수행원들 중 더욱 각별한 감회를 느꼈던 이들 가운데 한 사람이 바로 대하소설 〈태백산맥〉의 작가 조정래 씨였을 것입니다. 〈태백산맥〉 때문에 한때 국가보안법 위반으로 기소를 당하기도 했지만, 그의 책은 한국 성인 대부분이 읽었을 만큼 분단문학의 최고봉으로 꼽힙니다. 직접 북녘 땅을 밟은 뒤 김정일 국방위원장을 만난 그의 작가적 상상력은 한층 깊고 풍요로워질 것임에 틀림없습니다.

Taebaek Sanmaek Author and Chairman Kim Jong Il

Jo Jung-rae, the author of the epic novel Taebaek Sanmaek was perhaps the most deeply moved among the members of the South Korean delegation that visited the North along with President Roh Moo-hyun. Although the author was indicted for violating the National Security Law, the novel is considered to be the high point of pundan munhak (literature of division) and was read by most adults in Korea. One can only wonder what was going through his mind when he entered North Korea and met the North Korean leader face-to-face.

● ● ●

백화원(百花園)에는 붉은색 세이지를 비롯해 문자 그대로 100여 종의 꽃들이 예쁘게 피어 손님을 기다리고 있었습니다. 백화원 영빈관은 북한의 대표적인 국빈 숙소로 김대중 전 대통령과 고 정주영 현대그룹 명예회장이 이용했고, 장쩌민 중국 주석과 가네마루 신 일본 부총리가 묵었던 곳이기도 합니다. 노무현 대통령이 백화원에 만발한 꽃에 대해 질문하자 이곳 관계자가 자랑스러운 표정으로 답변하고 있습니다.

One Hundred Kinds of Flowers in Baekhwawon State Guesthouse

Literally, over a hundred different kinds of flowers, including red sage, decorated the State Guesthouse. Baekhwawon State Guesthouse is the lodging for state guests. Former President Kim Dae-jung stayed here, as did the late honorary president of the Hyundai Group Chung Ju Yung and other foreign dignitaries such as former President Jiang Zemin of China and former Deputy Prime Minister Kanemaru Shin of Japan.

● ● ●

남쪽의 국회의사당 격인 만수대 의사당을 방문한 노무현 대통령은 방명록에 이렇게 썼습니다.

"인민의 행복이…"는 고난에 찬 삶을 살면서도 나라의 기틀을 유지하고 있는 북녘 동포들에 대한 따뜻한 찬사일 수도 있고, 초대 받은 손님으로서의 의례적 표현일 수도 있습니다. 나중에 김정일 국방위원장이 여의도 국회의사당에 들러 '인민'을 '국민'으로 바꿔 똑같은 문구를 쓴다면 우리는 이를 어떻게 봐야 할까요?

"The Grand Hall Of the People's Sovereignty Where the Happiness of the People Originates."

That is what President Roh Moo-hyun wrote in the visitor's log on his visit to the Mansudae Assembly Hall, which is equivalent to the South Korean National Assembly. It could be interpreted as his warm-hearted praise for all North Koreans who are sustaining the nation while living under rigorous conditions, or his expression of courtesy as an invited guest. Sometime in the future, if North Korean leader Kim Jong Il comes and visits the National Assembly on Yeouido in the South and writes the same phrase, how would you feel?

인민의 행복이 나오는
인민주권의 전당

2007. 10. 2

대한민국
대통령 노무현

평화 위 번영의 한 반도시에
2000년 9월 18일 여름경 겨레행복 이희호

길은 핏줄이고 목숨줄이다

• • •

길은 단순히 특정 지점과 지점을 연결하는 공간이 아닙니다. 그것은 소원했던 관계를 복원하는 화해의 통로이자 새로운 삶을 불어넣을 수 있는 생명의 관(管)이며, 목숨을 살릴 수 있는 핏줄이기도 합니다. 반세기 동안 끊겼던 경의선 철도와 도로를 연결하는 일의 중요함도 바로 거기에 있습니다. 2000년 남북정상회담이 열린 지 석 달 뒤 김대중 전 대통령이 경의선 철도·도로 연결 기공식에서 철도 침목에 서명했습니다.

A Road is a Vein, a Lifeline

A road is not simply a line that connects point A to point B. It is a path to reconciliation, so that a broken relationship can be restored, a line that can imbue new life and even a symbolic vein that can carry blood to revive life. Reconnecting a road and the Seoul-Sinuiju Railroad Line that has been cut for almost a half a century is important for this reason. Three months after the 2000 South-North Korean Summit, former President Kim Dae-jung signs at a railroad tie during the groundbreaking ceremony to reconnect the Seoul-Sinuiju Line and a parallel road.

2부

대화

의사당 건물은 어디나 으리으리하다

● ● ●

서울의 여의도 국회의사당이나 평양의 만수대 의사당이나 할 것 없이 무릇 의사당은 웅장한 규모를
자랑하는 모양입니다. 만수대 의사당에서 '가장 높은 사람'인 김영남 최고인민회의 상임위원장의 안
내로 의사당 구내를 둘러보던 노무현 대통령이 이곳의 높은 천장을 가리키고 있습니다. 여의도가 높
은가, 만수대가 높은가.

Assembly Buildings Are Magnificent

Be it the National Assembly building on Yeouido or the Mansudae Assembly Hall in Pyongyang,
everyone seems to be proud of their magnificent size. President Roh points at the high ceiling during
his tour of the building, guided by Kim Young-nam, the Chairman of North Korea's Supreme People's
Assembly, where he presides over assembly meetings. I wonder which ceiling is higher; the one on
Yeouido or the one in the Mansudae?

여의도의 여야 회담이 아닙니다

• • •

여의도 국회의사당이 국회의원들의 '싸움터'로 종종 묘사되곤 하지만 그게 국회의사당의 본 모습은 아닙니다. 국가 운영의 핵심인 법이 만들어지고 통과되는 곳이지요. 법안의 제정과 심의를 위해 건강한 토론도 일상적으로 전개되는 것입니다. 만수대 의사당에서 열린 정치 분야 간담회에 참석한 대통합민주신당 김원기, 문희상 의원과 민주노동당 천영세 의원 등이 '카운터파트'인 최고인민회의 관계자들과 악수를 나누고 있습니다.

Not a Discussion Between the Government and Opposition Parties in Seoul
The National Assembly Hall in Seoul is often described as a "fighting the venue for deliberating and passing laws"—the essentials for running a nation. Constructive discussions on legislation take place there daily. In this photo, Senior United New Democratic Party members Kim Won-ki and Moon Hui-sang join Democratic Labor Party member Cheon Young-se in shaking hands with their counterparts from the People's Assembly before discussing issues at the Mansudae Assembly Hall in Pyongyang.

회담은 역시 '말로 하는 전쟁'

● ● ●

만수대 의사당 회담장에 마주 앉은 노무현 대통령과 김영남 최고인민회의 상임위원장. 얼굴에는 웃음을 띠고 있지만 실제 회담은 팽팽한 기싸움의 연속이었습니다. 김영남 위원장이 이른바 '3대 장애 요인'에 대해 무려 1시간 동안 장광설을 늘어놓자 노 대통령은 "들은 걸로 하겠다"고 말을 자르는가 하면 수행원들에게 "짐 싸서 돌아갈 준비를 하라"고 지시를 내리기도 했습니다. 성과를 내려면 우여곡절이 있게 마련입니다.

After All, a Summit is a War of Words

President Roh Moo-hyun and North Korea Supreme People's Assembly Chairman Kim Young-nam smile as they sit at the conference table in Mansudae Assembly Hall. However, the discussions on respective interests were intense. Chairman Kim spoke about the so-called "three major obstacle factors" for almost an hour, prompting President Roh to cut him off by saying he'd heard enough. He then ordered his delegation to pack up and get ready to leave. Results come only after many twists and turns.

목란관의 거친 파도!

• • •

김영남 최고인민회의 상임위원장이 노무현 대통령을 위해 마련한 공식 환영 만찬의 참석자들이 박수를 치고 있는 모습 뒤편으로 큰 파도가 일고 있는 대형 그림이 보입니다. 파도의 기세가 남과 북의 모든 대립과 불신을 단숨에 삼켜 버릴 듯합니다. 목란관은 북한의 국화인 목란에서 이름을 딴 국빈용 연회장으로, 2000년 김대중 전 대통령이 방북했을 때는 이곳에서 6·15 남북공동선언이 합의된 바 있습니다.

Foaming Waves in Mokran-gwan!

A massive ocean scene graces the wall behind the applauding guests at the official dinner given by North Korea Supreme People's Assembly Chairman Kim Young-nam for visiting President Roh. The force of the waves seems to be powerful enough to swallow any conflict and distrust that ever existed between the two Koreas. Mokran-gwan is a banquet restaurant for state guests and named after the magnolia, the official flower of North Korea. The June 15 North-South Joint Declaration was signed in this very restaurant when former President Kim Dae-jung visited Pyongyang in 2000.

오늘 같은 날은 한 잔 합시다!

● ● ●

대한민국을 '술 권하는 사회' 또는 '술 강요하는 사회'라고 비판하는 사람들이 있을 정도로, 권주(勸酒)는 종종 바람직하지 못한 행동으로 여겨집니다. 하지만 오늘같이 의미 깊은 날 어찌 한 잔 술이 없겠습니까? 목란관 공식 환영 만찬에서 노무현 대통령이 건배 제의를 하고 있습니다.

A Day Like Today Calls for a Toast!

Offering a drink in Korea can be inadvisable if you are a teetotaler. Some say that Korea is a society that invites you or even forces you to drink to excess. However, on a day as important as this, how could anyone not raise a glass? President Roh Moo-hyun offers a toast at the official welcoming dinner at Mokran-gwan.

일무이동!

● ● ●

백화원 영빈관에서 하룻밤을 보낸 노무현 대통령이 이튿날 수행원들과 정상회담 대책회의를 겸한 조찬을 함께 하면서 '일무이동(一無二同)'을 설파했습니다. 즉 남과 북은 '시차'가 없고, '음식'과 '언어'가 똑같아 다른 해외순방과는 달리 매우 편하다는 것이었습니다. 외국 출장을 자주 다니는 사람은 알 것입니다. 시차 없이, 입에 맞는 음식을 먹으며, 통역이 필요 없는 모국어로 회담을 한다는 게 얼마나 큰 행복인지를.

Not One, but Not Different!
After spending the night at the Baekhwawon State Guesthouse, President Roh Moo-hyun discusses the upcoming summit meeting with his staff over breakfast. He also spoke unexpectedly about Koreans being the same. That is, since the South and the North have no time difference and share the same language and cuisine, he said that his trip had been very comfortable, not like trips to other countries. Those who have traveled to other countries on business know how nice it is to eat familiar food, and talk in your mother tongue without the help of a translator, all without suffering from jet lag.

선물은 주어서 흐뭇하고 받아서 기쁘다

● ● ●

값어치나 규모에 관계없이 무릇 마음을 담아 건네는 선물은 소중한 법입니다. 노무현 대통령은 문화
예술 애호가로 알려진 김정일 국방위원장에게 드라마 〈대장금〉과 영화 〈올드보이〉, 〈취화선〉의 DVD
와 이를 시청할 수 있는 DVD 플레이어, 나전칠기로 된 십이장생도 병풍 등을 선물했습니다. 김정일
국방위원장은 노무현 대통령에게 함경도 칠보산 송이버섯 4톤을 건넸습니다. 북은 남의 문화예술을
감상하고, 남은 북의 영양식을 즐겼습니다. 서로의 몸과 마음을 건강하게 한 셈입니다.

Gifts: Glad to Give, Happy to Receive

Presents that come from the heart are priceless, regardless of their monetary value or size. National
Defense Commission Chairman Kim Jong Il is well known as a movie buff. President Roh Moo-hyun's
presents for him included DVDs of the dramas Dae Jang Geum, Old Boy and Strokes of Fire; a DVD
player; and a folding screen featuring the 12 longevity symbols in mother-of-pearl. National Defense
Commission Chairman Kim gave President Roh four tons of naturally grown pine mushrooms from Mt.
Chilbo in Hamgyeong-do (province). The North could enjoy culture and arts from the South, while the
South got some healthy gourmet cuisine from the North. Each side enriched the other.

중요한 일을 앞두고 터뜨리는 파안대소

● ● ●

남북정상회담과 같은 중대한 일에 임할수록 활짝 웃으며 상대방에게 진심 어린 덕담을 건네는 것이 필요합니다. 본격적인 회담을 앞둔 노무현 대통령과 김정일 국방위원장이 뒤편에 걸려 있는 그림 속의 힘찬 파도와도 같이 크게 웃고 있습니다. 두 정상은 회담 내내, 그리고 회담이 끝난 뒤에도 따뜻한 분위기를 연출했습니다.

A Lighthearted Moment Before a Major Occasion

Good wishes and smiles for one another are just the right thing for participants in an occasion such as this. As the official inter-Korean summit nears, President Roh and his North Korean counterpart, Chairman Kim, enjoy a laugh as sweeping as the powerful waves in the painting behind them. This friendly atmosphere was maintained throughout the meeting as well as afterwards.

마주 보는 눈길이 따뜻하다

● ● ●

드디어 회담 테이블에 마주 앉은 남북의 정상. 그런데 서로를 바라보는 두 사람의 시선이 오래된 친구처럼 정겹습니다. 너무 분위기가 화기애애해서 였을까요? 오후에 열린 제2차 회의에서 김정일 국방위원장은 노무현 대통령에게 "하루 더 묵고 가시라"며 회담 일정 연장을 제의했습니다. 결국 회담 연장은 '없던 일'이 됐지만 지나치게 좋았던 분위기로 인한 해프닝이 아니었을까요?

Warmly Facing Each Other

Finally, the leaders of the two Koreas face each other at the conference table. The air of congeniality—like old friends—is reassuring. During the second session in the afternoon, Chairman Kim invited President Roh to extend his stay one more day. The suggestion was eventually dropped, but it was very likely the result of the friendlier-than-expected mood.

'보통명사'가 된 옥류관

● ● ●

평양, 원산, 두만강, 압록강, 백두산, 금강산 등 북한의 지명을 제외한 고유명사 가운데 남녘 사람들에게도 친숙한 이름 가운데 하나가 바로 옥류관일 것입니다. 대동강 기슭 옥류바위에 있는 음식점으로 평양냉면, 대동강 숭어국 등이 유명한 옥류관은 서울을 비롯한 남녘 곳곳에 똑같은 이름의 냉면집을 낳았습니다. 이름만 옥류관이 아닌 음식 맛과 정성까지도 '원조 대동강 옥류관'과 똑같은 수많은 옥류관이 전국 곳곳에 생겨나면 얼마나 좋을까요?

Okryukwan, Now a Common Noun

South Koreans are familiar with many North Korean place names—Pyongyang, Wonsan, Tumen River, Amnok River, Mt. Baekdu and Mt. Geumgang. During the summit Okryukwan was added to the list. Situated by Okryu Rock on the bank of the Daedonggang (river), Okryukwan is a restaurant renowned for its Pyongyang Raengmyeon (cold noodles), and Daedonggang Mullet Soup. Cold noodle restaurants in the South are taking the name from this famous restaurant. One can only hope that some of these other Okryukwans are on a par with this one for flavor and wholehearted commitment to the dish.

● ● ●

노무현 대통령이 수행원들과 기자단을 위해 마련한 옥류관 오찬에서 정몽구 현대기아자동차 회장과
이철 철도공사 사장, 최태원 SK그룹 회장(앞줄 왼쪽부터)의 표정이 흥미롭습니다. 정 회장과 이 사
장은 진지한 표정으로 노 대통령의 격려사를 듣고 있는 반면 최 회장은 디지털 카메라로 오찬장의
이모저모를 담기에 여념이 없습니다.

Young CEO with a Flair for Reporting

President Roh hosted a luncheon at Okryukwan for the members of his delegation and reporters.
Hyundai-Kia Motors Chairman Chung Mong-gu, Korea Railroad Corp. President Lee Chul and SK Group
Chairman Chey Tae-won (front row, from the left) show interest in what is going on. While the other
two listen attentively to President Roh's address, Chairman Chey is absorbed in taking pictures with
his digital camera.

남과 북의 국수 맛은 우열을 가릴 수 없다!

● ● ●

남북정상회담 2차 회의 직전 김정일 국방위원장은 "옥류관에서 국수를 드셨다는데 평양 국수와 서울 국수 가운데 어떤 게 맛있느냐"고 물었습니다. 노 대통령은 "맛있게 먹었다. 평양 국수 맛이 진한 것 같다"고 대답했습니다. 남북의 국수가 서로 특장이 있을 뿐이라는 현답(賢答)을 내놓은 셈입니다. 따지고 보면 남과 북 사이에서 일도양단식의 승부를 낼 수 없는 것이 어디 국수뿐이겠습니까? 서로의 고유한 가치가 있을 뿐 기계적 승패를 가릴 수 없는 것들이 아주 많겠지요.

Hard to Tell which Tastes Better, Southern or Northern Noodles

Right before the second summit session, National Defense Commission Chairman Kim asked President Roh, "You've tried the noodles at Okryukwan. Which was tastier, the noodles in Pyongyang or in Seoul? President Roh replied, "They were both delicious, but the Pyongyang variety has a more intense flavor" His prudent answer implied that the noodles of both Koreas were simply different. After all, noodles are not the only inter-Korean issue upon which we cannot pass a clear-cut judgment. Many things on each side have their own merits and defy an automatic declaration of victory or defeat by the other.

'아리랑 고개'를 넘어라!

• • •

회담이 열리기 전부터 남쪽 일각에서는 〈아리랑〉이 북한 체제를 일방적으로 선전하는 공연이라는 이유로 '관람 불가론'을 지폈습니다. 그러나 노무현 대통령은 능라도 5·1경기장에서 열린 〈아리랑〉 공연을 예정대로 관람했습니다. 노무현 대통령이 입장하자 10만여 명의 대관중은 일제히 환호성과 함께 박수를 보냈고, 노무현 대통령은 꽃다발을 번쩍 들어 올리며 화답했습니다. '아리랑 고개'를 단숨에 넘어선 것이었습니다.

Crossing Arirang Hill

Prior to the summit, some in the South voiced strong objections to the President's plan to watch the Arirang mass performance because it was North Korean government propaganda. But President Roh attended the performance as scheduled at the May Day Stadium in Neungrado. When he entered the stadium, the crowd of over 100,000 people greeted him with thunderous applause and cheers. President Roh responded by holding up a bouquet high in the air and waving it. He went over Arirang Hill (as the song goes) just like that.

〈아리랑〉은 〈아리랑〉으로 관람하면 된다

● ● ●

〈아리랑〉은 과연 어떤 작품일까요? 북한 현대사를 노래, 무용, 체조, 교예의 종합 예술로 형상화한 〈아리랑〉은 과연 북한 체제의 선전물일까요? 아니면 완성도 높은 예술작품일까요? 정답은 '둘 다' 입니다. 어떤 시대, 어떤 체제의 문화에도 당대의 현실이 반영돼 있습니다. 우리는 〈아리랑〉을 통해 북한이 헤쳐 온 어려움과 지금 처해 있는 상황, 그리고 북측의 정치 이념과 그들이 생각하는 역사 인식 등을 한눈에 읽을 수 있습니다.

Seeing Arirang for What It Is

What is this mass performance Arirang about? When the modern history of the North is played out in songs, music and acrobatics, is it North Korean government propaganda or just a highly perfected piece of art? The answer is: both. Culture created under any government reflects the reality of the times. The Arirang mass performance gave a glimpse of the difficulties that North Koreans have gone through and still face, as well as their agony and pride.

〈아리랑〉의 한반도에는 분단의 흔적이 없다

● ● ●

〈아리랑〉에는 북한이 평소에도 강조하는 '민족 단결'이나 '우리 민족끼리' 같은 구호가 적극적으로 반영돼 있습니다. 수많은 여성들이 한복을 입고 연출한 한반도의 모습이 인상적입니다. 동해 맨 오른쪽 울릉도와 독도는 다섯 명의 여성이 연출했습니다. 한반도의 허리에는 아무런 경계선도 보이지 않습니다.

Korean Peninsula Portrayed in Arirang without Division

Northern slogans such as "National Solidarity" and "By the Korean People Ourselves" were enthusiastically presented at the Arirang performance. Particularly impressive was the shape of the Korean Peninsula formed by women wearing traditional Korean dresses. Ulleungdo and Dokdo (islands) on the right side were created by five women. But no dividing line crossed the midsection of the Peninsula.

● ● ●

노무현 대통령이 주최한 평양 인민문화궁전 답례 만찬에서 판소리 〈사랑가〉와 〈벗님가〉의 구성진 가락이 울려 퍼졌습니다. 만찬이 끝날 무렵 마련된 간단한 여흥 자리에서 안숙선 명창이 판소리를 부르자 도올 김용옥 세명대 석좌교수가 북채를 잡고 즉석에서 고수 역할을 맡았습니다. 어화, 남북의 벗님네들, 왕후장상이 부럽지 않고, 세상 풍진이 남이로구나. 이렁성 저렁성 지내여 보세! 어화 둥둥 내 사랑아.

South and North Are Friends

The touching melody of Korean pansori (traditional long, solo epic song) "Song of Love" and "Song for a Dear Friend" resonates through the People's Palace of Culture, where President Roh hosted a reciprocal dinner. Pansori master Ahn Sook-sun performed during an interlude just as the dinner was coming to an end, and Semyeong University Professor Kim Yong-ok (a.k.a Dohl) spontaneously volunteered to accompany her on the drum. "U-Hwa, dear friends from the South and the North. I envy not royalty nor titled nobility; worldly troubles are only for others. We will pass our time, in a simple and friendly fashion! U-Hwa-Dung-Dung, my beloved."

남북이 합치면 '평화'가 굴러간다

● ● ●

남포의 자동차 조립 공장인 평화자동차는 남북 최초의 합영회사라는 상징성에 걸맞게 '평화' 라는 이름을 붙이고 있습니다. 평화자동차를 방문한 노무현 대통령 일행 가운데 자신의 '전공 분야' 인 자동차에 대해 자신감 있는 표정으로 얘기하는 정몽구 현대기아자동차 회장의 표정이 이채롭습니다.

Peace Reigns When the South and the North Come Together

Pyonghwa Motors, an automobile assembling facility located in Nampo, has a name that matches its highly symbolic presence as the first joint corporation between the South and the North. Among the delegates accompanying President Roh Moo-hyun to visit Pyonghwa Motors, Chung Mong-gu, the Chairman of Hyundai-Kia Motors Group, stands out as he talks about his 'major area' of automobiles, with a look of confidence on his face.

'평화' 만드느라 고생 많습니다

● ● ●

남포의 자동차 조립공장인 평화자동차에서 자동차가 많이 생산되면 될수록 그만큼 남북의 평화도 더
왕성하게 굴러가는 셈입니다. 평화자동차를 방문한 노무현 대통령이 현장 근로자의 등을 두드리고
있습니다. '평화 만들기'의 노고에 대한 따뜻한 격려인 셈입니다.

Keep up the Good Work to Make "Peace"
During a tour of Pyonghwa (Peace) Motors, an automobile assembly operation in Nampo, President
Roh is patting a worker on the back. The more vehicles that are manufactured here, the better the
chance for inter-Korean peace. The President's warm pep talk expresses appreciation to the workers
for their endeavors to "make peace."

서해갑문, 끝없이 길구나!

• • •

엄청난 규모의 인공 건축물 앞에 서면 새삼 인간 의지와 노력의 위대함을 떠올리게 됩니다. 서해갑
문도 그 대표적인 경우라 하겠습니다. 노무현 대통령이 방명록에 "인민은 위대하다"라고 썼던 것도
바로 그러한 이유였을 것입니다. 남포항의 접안 능력을 높이고 농업·공업용수를 확보하기 위해 5년
간의 대역사(大役事) 끝에 1986년에 준공된 길이 8km의 이 거대한 제방은 북한의 으뜸가는 자랑거
리이기도 합니다.

West Sea Floodgate Stretches Endlessly!

Enormous construction projects show how much can be achieved through human resolve and effort.
The Seohae (West Sea) Floodgate is a good example. Perhaps that is why President Roh wrote "The
people are great" in the visitor's log. The 8km structure is a source of great pride for North Koreans,
completed in 1986 after five years of construction. It ensures a water supply for agriculture and
industry and improves the approach for ships to Nampo Port.

● ● ●

'한국식 관광'의 특색 가운데 하나가 경관이나 유물은 제대로 보지 않더라도 그것을 배경으로 사진 찍는 일만은 결코 빠뜨리지 않는다는 것입니다. 정상회담의 공식 일정이라 하더라도 관광은 관광. 서해갑문까지 왔는데 어찌 사진 한 장 찍지 않을 수 있을까요? 서해갑문은 웅장하고 사진은 영원합니다.

A Keepsake Photo at Seohae Floodgate is a Must

Koreans on tour typically care less about the scenery or tourist attractions than they do about taking a commemorative photo with the sight in the background. A tour is a tour, even during an official schedule for a summit meeting. A photo opportunity at Seohae Floodgate is too good to pass up. The area is a grand sight, and the picture will bring lasting memories.

우람하여라, 광개토대왕릉비여!

● ● ●

광개토대왕의 웅혼한 기상은 만주 지린성 지안현뿐만 아니라 평양에도 서려 있었습니다. 북한 최대의 박물관인 평양 조선중앙역사박물관에는 구석기 시대부터 근대에 이르기까지 10만 점이 넘는 유물이 전시돼 있는데, 그 가운데 가장 큰 자랑거리가 바로 광개토대왕릉비입니다. 물론 이 비석은 모형이지만 정교함과 웅장함이 결코 '오리지널'에 뒤지지 않습니다.

The Hallowed Stele of King Gwanggaeto the Great

The spirit of King Gwanggaeto can be found not just in Ji'an, Jilin Province in Manchuria, but also in Pyongyang, North Korea. The Central Museum of History is the largest museum in the North, with over 100,000 artifacts on display that can be traced as far back as the Paleolithic era. One of the proudest exhibits is the Stele of King Gwanggaeto the Great. Of course, this marker is only a replica, but it is faithful to the original in both detail and enormous size.

문화예술인들은 역시 예술에 관심이 많다

● ● ●

만수대 창작사는 북한 최고, 최대의 집단 미술 창작 단체로 1,000명이 넘는 화가들이 소속돼 있습니다. 만수대 창작사를 방문한 신경림 시인, 문학평론가 백낙청 교수, 도올 김용옥 교수 등 문화예술인들이 이곳에 전시된 각종 작품을 둘러보고 있습니다.

Artists Surely Have a Special Interest in Arts

The Mansudae Art Studio is the oldest and largest group dedicated to collective creation of art works and has over 1,000 members. South Korean artists visiting the Mansudae Art Studio, including poet Shin Kyung-rim, literary critic and professor Baek Nak-cheong and Prof. Kim Yong-ok, view the artworks on display.

음악의 아름다움에는 남북이 따로 없다

● ● ●

남북정상회담 특별 수행원들이 방문한 김원균 명칭 평양음악대학 학생들이 기악과 성악을 공부하고 있습니다. 〈김일성 장군의 노래〉 등을 작곡한 김원균의 이름을 딴 이 대학에는 800여 명의 학생들이 800여 명의 교수들로부터 배우고 있습니다. 성악 수업 시간에 한복을 입은 여학생들과 정장을 한 남학생들의 모습이 이채롭습니다.

No National Divide when It Comes to Beautiful Music

Delegates to the summit visit the Kim Won Gyun Pyongyang Conservatory, where the students are practicing vocal and instrumental pieces. This conservatory is named after the composer Kim Won-gyun, who wrote such pieces as the "Song For General Kim Il-sung." It has over 800 professors teaching more than 800 students. Of particular interest is how the girls are dressed in traditional Korean dresses and the boys look in their formal suits.

3부

약속

● ● ●

회담을 하는 동안 때로는 상대에게 덕담을 건네기도 하고, 때로는 한 치의 양보 없이 치열한 논전(論戰)을 벌이기도 합니다. 이러한 화전(和戰)의 총체적 결과가 바로 합의문이라는 한 장의 종이 위에 나타납니다. 노무현 대통령과 김정일 국방위원장이 회담을 끝낸 뒤 개운한 표정으로 합의문에 서명하고 있습니다.

Summit Meeting Bears Fruit with a Joint Declaration

During the talks, they exchange friendly remarks, and sometimes engage in heated arguments without yielding an inch. The comprehensive results of such a war of words are presented on a piece of paper at the end, as a joint declaration. After the summit, President Roh Moo-hyun and National Defense Commission Chairman Kim Jong Il sign the Summit Declaration with a rather relieved look on their faces.

열 번의 합의보다는 단 한 번의 실천이 중요하다

● ● ●

남북 관계에서 우리가 경험적으로 알고 있는 사실이 바로 이것이기도 합니다. 열 번, 백 번의 합의도 단 한 번의 약속 파기와 불이행으로 어려움을 겪었던 일이 적지 않았기 때문입니다. 합의문 서명과 교환을 마친 노무현 대통령과 김정일 국방위원장이 맞잡은 손을 번쩍 들어 올리고 있습니다. 그것은 "이제는 실천입니다"라는 서로에 대한 맹세이기도 했을 것입니다.

One Action Is More Important than Ten Agreements.
That is a fact that we came to learn through experience in terms of the inter-Korean relationship. Our experience tells us that ten or even one hundred agreements can be made, but just a single break or breach of a promise can make for difficult times afterward. After exchanging copies of the signed Summit Declaration, President Roh and Chairman Kim join hands and raise them high. This gesture appears to be a promise to each other, saying "Now, it's time for action."

술은 역시 '원샷'으로 마셔야 제 맛이 난다

● ● ●

빨리 취한다는, 그래서 건강에 좋지 않다는 단점에도 불구하고 술은 단숨에 들이켜야 할 때가 있습니다. 김정일 국방위원장이 노무현 대통령을 위해 마련한 송별 오찬에서 두 사람이 포도주를 '원샷'으로 들이켜고 있습니다. 노무현 대통령은 '1차 시기'에서 술을 잔에 조금 남겨 '판정패'를 당했습니다.

Drinks Taste Best when Downed All at Once

It may get you drunk faster and be bad for your health, but there are times when one needs to finish a drink in one shot. At a farewell luncheon hosted by Chairman Kim Jong Il for President Roh Moo-hyun, the two leaders drink wine in one-shot. President Roh lost the first round, having left a little bit in his glass.

만나면 또 헤어져야 한다

● ● ●

사람과 사람이 만났다가 헤어지는 일은 언제나 아쉽고 섭섭한 법입니다. 더욱이 남북정상회담과 같이 강도 높은 만남 뒤에는 더욱 그러할 것입니다. 2박 3일의 평양 체류를 끝내고 돌아가는 노무현 대통령과 보내는 김정일 국방위원장의 얼굴에도 그 같은 사람 사는 일의 본새가 그대로 나타나고 있습니다.

Meeting Is the Other Side of Parting

Bidding farewell to someone you know is always sad. It is all the more so when it comes after such a highly charged meeting as the inter-Korean summit. The looks on the faces of President Roh, who is about to leave after three days and two nights in Pyongyang, and Chairman Kim reveal the same feelings that most everyone has on meeting and parting.

한라산과 백두산이 흙과 물로 합쳐지네

• • •

한라산의 흙은 백두산의 흙과, 백록담의 물은 천지의 물과 결국 하나가 됐습니다. 노무현 대통령과 김영남 상임위원장은 남측에서 가져온 반송(盤松) 한 그루를 평양 중앙식물원에 함께 심으면서 남과 북을 대표하는 산의 흙을 합토(合土)하고, 그 산 꼭대기에 고여 있는 물을 주었습니다. 남북 영산(靈山)의 흙과 물을 한 몸에 받았으니 어찌 우람하게 자라지 않을 수 있을까요.

Soil and Water from Mt. Halla and Mt. Baekdu Come Together as One

Soil from Mt. Halla in South Korea was blended with soil from Mt. Baekdu in North Korea, and water from the lakes atop those two peaks were mixed as well. The mixtures were then used when President Roh Moo-hyun and North Korea's Supreme People's Assembly Chairman Kim Young-nam planted a pine tree that the South delegates brought to the Pyongyang Central Botanic Garden. Now that the sapling is blessed with soil and water from the sacred mountains of the South and North, it will surely grow into a magnificent tree.

코 리 아
KOREA

한반도기는 남북을 합친 깃발!

● ● ●

국기는 국가 정체성의 최고 상징물입니다. 대한민국의 국기인 태극기와 조선민주주의인민공화국의 국기인 인공기(공식 명칭은 홍람오각별기)는 명칭과 존재만으로도 상대에게 대결 의식을 심어 왔습니다. 한반도기는 바로 이러한 현실의 절묘한 타협이자 절충인 셈입니다. 올림픽 등 국제 스포츠 행사에서 남북한이 한반도기를 앞세우고 동시에 입장하는 모습은 이제 익숙한 광경이 됐습니다.

The Unification Flag Symbolizes a Unified Peninsula!

A national flag is the supreme symbol of national sovereignty. The names and the very presence of the national flags of the Republic of Korea and Democratic People's Republic of Korea have always generated feelings of confrontation. The Korean Unification Flag is an exquisite compromise and solution for this troubling reality. Now, we are all familiar with the athletes from the two sides making their entry holding a Unification Flag in major international sports events, including the Olympic Games.

1 더하기 1은 2가 아니다

● ● ●

남북이 하나로 합치면 수십 곱절의 위력을 발휘합니다. 1991년 4월 일본 지바에서 열린 제41회 세계 탁구선수권대회 여자 복식에서 남의 현정화(사진 오른쪽)와 북의 이분희가 주축이 된 남북 단일팀은 막강 중국을 꺾고 우승을 차지했습니다. 국기 게양대에는 한반도기가 올라가고 국가로는 〈아리랑〉이 울려 퍼졌습니다. 민단, 총련 할 것 없이 재일동포들도 눈물을 흘리며 〈아리랑〉을 따라 불렀습니다.

One Plus One Does Not Equal Just Two

Uniting the South and the North can bring results ten times larger than what the two sides are separately. In April 1991, at the 41st International Ping Pong Championship in Chiba, Japan, a united Korean team, with Hyun Jeong-hwa(right) representing the South and Lee Bun-hui representing the North, defeated the powerful Chinese team and won the championship. The Korean Unification Flag was raised above the medal stand, and Arirang was played as the national anthem. Koreans living in Japan, both from Mindan (the pro-Seoul Korean Residents Union in Japan) and Chongryon (the pro-Pyongyang General Association of Korean Residents in Japan), sang along with tears in their eyes.

남과 북이 하나 되면 세계 최강도 물리친다

● ● ●

축구 신동 마라도나를 낳은 아르헨티나는 브라질과 함께 명실 공히 세계 최강의 축구 왕국입니다. 그러나 1991년 제6회 세계청소년축구대회에서 남북 단일팀은 아르헨티나의 높은 벽을 단숨에 무너 뜨렸습니다. 남의 철저한 수비와 북의 멋진 공격이 환상의 조합을 이룬 결과였습니다. 여자 탁구 남 북 단일팀이 일본 지바에서 우승의 쾌거를 거둔 지 불과 두 달 만이었습니다.

A United Korea Can Defeat the World's Strongest

Argentina, the home of the soccer genius Maradona, is considered one of the world's most powerful soccer empires along with Brazil. But in 1991, at the Sixth World Youth Soccer Tournament, the South-North unified team defeated the superpower Argentina almost effortlessly. The fantastic unity of the tight defense skill of the South and the amazing offensive skill of the North were what made the outcome possible. It came only two months after the united South-North ping-pong team won the championship in Chiba, Japan.

0-0이 좋다!

● ● ●

이겨도 기쁘고, 져도 흐뭇하고, 비기면 더욱더 의미 있습니다. 무릇 친선경기에서 두 눈에 핏발 세울 필요가 뭐 있겠습니까. 하물며 남북한 동포애를 나누는 경기에서야 두말할 나위도 없겠죠. 남북 청소년 친선축구대회에서 점수판에 나타난 0-0이란 숫자가 정겹습니다.

We Love a 0-0 Tie!

Glad to win, and pleased to lose. Even a tie means a lot to all of us. In friendly games, why should anybody be bloodthirsty for victory? All the more so when it is a friendly game to share the brotherhood between the two Koreas. The scoreboard that reads 0-0 is heartwarming at the South-North Youth Friendly Soccer Tournament.

남북 청소년 U-17 축구대표팀
친선경기
5
남측 vs 북측
남측 전 북측
0 0

헤어지기 아쉽다면 박수 치고 꽃 흔들자

● ● ●

2박 3일의 일정을 마치고 평양을 떠나는 노무현 대통령 내외가 조국통일 3대 기념현장 기념탑 앞에서 열린 공식 환송식에서 환송객들을 향해 손을 흔들며 고마움을 표시하고 있습니다. 두 사람의 표정에 서운한 기색이 역력합니다. 꽃을 흔들거나 박수를 치며 남녘의 대통령을 보내는 평양 시민들의 표정에서 아쉬움이 엿보입니다.

Applause and Flower Waving Instead of Sorrow on Leaving

President Roh Moo-hyun and the First Lady have finished their visit of three days and two nights, and are ready to leave Pyongyang. They attend the official farewell ceremony in front of the Monument to the Three-point Charter of National Reunification and show their appreciation by waving to the people who came to see them off. The expressions on their faces clearly show they are sorry to leave. The Pyongyang citizens wave flowers or applaud to express their reluctance to see the President from the South leaving.

'메이드 인 개성'은 결국 '메이드 인 코리아'이다

• • •

개성공단에서 만든 물건은 대한민국 제품인가? 조선민주주의인민공화국 제품인가? 둘 다 맞습니다. 남쪽의 자본과 북측의 노동력이 합쳐진 작품이기 때문입니다. 동시에 둘 다 틀렸습니다. 어느 한쪽만의 일방적인 요소가 생산을 결정하지 않기 때문입니다. 결국 '메이드 인 개성'은 남과 북을 합친 '메이드 인 코리아' 입니다. 노무현 대통령 일행이 개성공단 작업 현장을 둘러보고 있습니다.

"Made in Gaeseong" is "Made in Korea" After All

Are the products from Gaeseong Industrial Complex made in the Republic of Korea or made in the Democratic People's Republic of Korea? The answer is, they are both, since they are the results of a partnership between the capital of the South and the labor of the North. But at the same time, they are neither, because production has not been carried out by just one side. Therefore, "Made in Gaeseong" has to be considered the same as "Made in Korea," a joint effort of the South and the North. President Roh Moo-hyun and his delegates are having a tour around the Gaeseong Industrial Complex.

●●●

개성공단인가, 개성백화점인가? 전자제품에서부터 화장품, 고급 운동화, 하이힐 등 개성공단에서 만들어 내는 제품들은 실로 다양합니다. 노무현 대통령이 공단 구내 전시관에 진열된 온갖 제품들을 바라보며 미소를 짓고 있습니다.

Anything Can Be Found in the Gaeseong Industrial Complex

Is this Gaeseong Industrial Complex, or Gaeseong Department Store? The products found in Gaeseong were diverse, from appliances to cosmetics, luxurious sneakers, and high heels. President Roh smiles as he looks at the various products on display in the exhibition hall of the industrial complex.

● ● ●

역시 동심(童心)은 어른들의 마음보다는 울림이 큽니다. 똑같이 〈우리의 소원〉을 불러도 아이들의 노래가 가슴속을 훨씬 더 깊이 파고듭니다. 정상회담을 마치고 돌아온 노무현 대통령 일행이 경기도 파주시 도라산 남북출입사무소에서 열린 환영 행사에서 아이들과 함께 〈우리의 소원〉을 소리 높여 부르고 있습니다.

Singing a Song of Unification with the Children

Surely, innocent children's hearts have greater resonance than those of adults. They are singing the same "Our Wish is Unification" song, but the sound of the children's voices reaches deeper into our hearts. President Roh Moo-hyun and his staff are singing "Our Wish is Unification" together with children at a welcoming ceremony hosted at the cross-border point in Paju, Gyeonggi Province.

평화를 다지는 길
번영으로 가는 길

ⓒ사진공동취재단

송도삼절(松都三絶) 가운데 하나만 남았으니

●●●

옛 시조에도 나오듯이 '인걸은 간 데 없어도 산천은 의구한' 법입니다. 바로 박연폭포가 그러합니다. 조선시대에는 송도삼절(松都三絶), 즉 지금의 개성인 송도의 세 가지 뛰어난 존재로서 명기(名妓) 황진이, 대학자 서경덕, 그리고 박연폭포를 꼽았습니다. 지금 황진이와 서경덕은 이름 석 자를 남기고 역사와 전설이 되었지만, 박연폭포만은 여전히 거대한 물줄기를 내리쏟고 있습니다. 이제 개성 관광까지 가능하게 됐다니, 남아 있는 송도일절(松都一絶)을 눈앞에서 볼 수 있게 됐습니다.

Symbols of the Ancient City of Gaeseong

Bakyeon Waterfalls was one of the three symbols of 16th century Gaeseong, an ancient city called Songdo at the time. The other two symbols were human—the first being Hwang Jin-i, a famous gisaeng (female hostess and companion) and poetess, and Seo Gyeong-deok, a renowned philosopher and teacher. As one Joseon Kingdom poem says, "Wherever Have All the People Gone/The Mountain and River Remain the Same." Well, at least one of the three is still there today as shown in the photo, and the good news is that Gaeseong, just to the north of the inter-Korean border, will soon be open to South Korean tourists.

절경 중의 절경이니 왕중왕이로소이다!

● ● ●

금강산은 우리나라의 가장 아름다운 명승지 중 한 곳으로 꼽힙니다. 그 가운데서도 가장 빼어난 절경이 바로 만물상입니다. 저마다 다른 일만여 개의 형상이 아름다운 자태를 뽐내고 있는데, 보는 각도와 위치에 따라 천변만화(千變萬化)의 모습을 보여준다는 것이지요. 남북관계도 만물상을 닮으면 좋겠습니다. 지난날처럼 단 하나의 고정된 틀에 얽매여 서로를 바라보지 말고 상대의 형편과 사정에 따라 따뜻하게 배려하는 것 말입니다.

Unmatched Picturesque Scenery

Mt. Geumgang is rated as one of the most scenic places in Korea. Manmulsang (Rocks of Ten-thousands Features) stands out by far. Huge rocks, each with a different shape, combine to create an enchanting aura displaying diverse configurations depending on which angle or position they are seen from. I wish inter-Korean relations to be like kaleidoscopic rocks. Each side needs to show flexibility by going beyond old-fashioned ways, thus being more considerate of each other by taking into account the fluid situations facing them both.

Ⓒ이정수

ⓒ이정수

민족의 물줄기, 여기서 발원하다!

● ● ●

백두산은 한반도에서 가장 높은 산이라는, 단순한 지리학적 지식의 대상이 아닙니다. 그것은 한민족의 시원(始原)과 웅혼한 기상, 통일의 염원까지를 망라하는 민족사적 상징이기도 합니다. 어느 맑은 가을날, 백두산의 높고 웅장한 봉우리가 푸르고 높은 하늘에 닿아 있습니다. 남북정상회담을 통해 백두산 직항로 개설이 합의된 만큼 이제 먼 길을 돌아서 그곳에 갈 필요가 없게 됐습니다.

Physical Source of the Spirit of the Korean Nation

Mt. Baekdu represents more than the highest mountain on the Korean Peninsula. It is the very symbol of the Korean people, the beginning of the nation, their spirit and their desire to become one again. One autumn day, the summit of the magnificent Mt. Baekdu seems to touch the high blue skies. The inter-Korean summit agreed to inaugurate direct flights from Seoul to the mountain in the North, the first air route linking the two Koreas.

동해의 일출은 변함이 없다

● ● ●

아침이면 한반도의 동쪽 바다에서 해가 솟아오릅니다. 그것은 반세기의 분단 상황 아래서도 단 한번의 어김이 없었습니다. 해금강에서 바라본 동해의 일출이 가슴 벅찬 장관을 연출하고 있습니다. 동해의 태양은 앞으로도 영원히 한반도를 어루만질 것입니다.

The Sunrise in the East Sea Remains the Same

In the morning, the sun rises over the East Sea off the Korean Peninsula as it has always done. And that has not changed over the last half century when the nation has been divided. The sunrise over the East Sea, as seen from the Sea Geumgang is a never-ending scene that excites all Korean hearts.

ⓒ이정수

흙과 흙이 합쳐지고,
물과 물이 하나되네

초판 1쇄 발행 2007년 12월 26일

기획 | 국정홍보처
글 | 손동우
사진 | 2007 남북정상회담 사진공동취재단

펴낸곳 | 바다출판사
펴낸이 | 김인호

주소 | 서울시 마포구 서교동 403-21 서홍빌딩 4층
전화 | 02-322-3885(편집부), 02-322-3575(마케팅부)
팩스 | 02-322-3858
E - mail | badabooks@dreamwiz.com
출판등록일 | 1996년 5월 8일
등록번호 | 제10-1288호

ISBN 978-89-5561-412-1 03300